A New True Book

VIETNAM

By Karen Jacobsen

Flag of Vietnam

CHILDRENS PRESS ®

CHICAGO

THE NATION

Vietnam is in Southeast Asia. It has a long and curving shape, like the letter *S*. Vietnam lies on the east coast of a large peninsula called Indochina.

Three countries share borders with Vietnam: China in the north, Laos in the west, and Cambodia (or Kampuchea) in the southwest.

Three bodies of water— the Gulf of Thailand, the

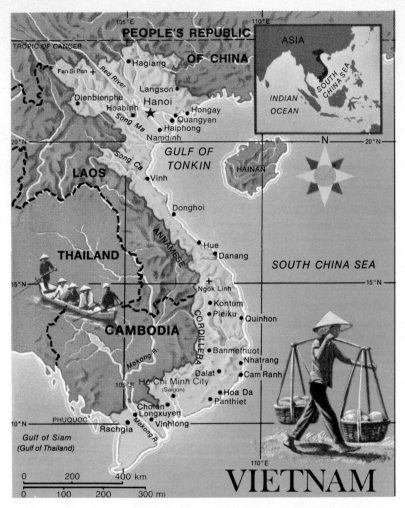

VIETNAM

Vietnam is 1,030 miles long. It is widest in the north—as much as 380 miles across from east to west. But in its middle, Vietnam is very narrow. It is as little as 40 miles across.

South China Sea, and the Gulf of Tonkin—wash Vietnam's shores.

In the busy city of Hanoi, people ride the trolley (below left) to the market (above). A man (below right) brings his chickens to the market.

Hanoi is in the northern part of Vietnam.

Today, Vietnam is called the Socialist Republic of Vietnam. Its capital city is Hanoi.

The National Assembly makes Vietnam's laws and chooses Vietnam's prime minister and deputy ministers. The leaders of the government are members of the Vietnamese Communist party.

7

A tea plantation in the mountains of Vietnam

THE LAND

Vietnam has four geographic regions: mountains, long coastal lowlands, and two large, fertile river deltas.

A long chain of mountains and plateaus covers about 75 percent of Vietnam. The mountains stretch from China southward almost to Ho Chi Minh City. They are from 3,000 to 10,000 feet

The coastal lowland is sandwiched between Vietnam's southern mountains and the South China Sea. Some areas have small freshwater streams and rivers. Hue

The seacoast at Nha Trang, Vietnam

The city of Da Nang is a fishing port on the central coast of Vietnam. Like Hanoi, it has a busy street market.

and Da Nang are the main cities on the central coast.

Mighty rivers form the two deltas. The Red River flows from China, through northern Vietnam, and into the Gulf of Tonkin. Its water carries the land's

The Mekong River carries topsoil from upriver to the Mekong Delta.

red soil downriver to the Red River Delta. The delta is the largest farming area in northern Vietnam. Its main crop is rice. Hanoi and Haiphong are the region's chief cities.

The Mekong River starts

Rice farmers in the Mekong River Delta, which is the home of more than 30 million people. More than 1,000 miles of canals crisscross the delta.

in Tibet, China. It flows south, through Laos, Thailand, and Cambodia before reaching southern Vietnam and splitting into several branches. The Mekong River Delta region is Vietnam's richest rice-growing area.

15

THE PEOPLE

More than 74 million people live in Vietnam today. About 90 percent of the people are Vietnamese.

The Vietnamese live in the Red River and Mekong deltas and along the coast of Vietnam. Some are city people. Many more live in villages and work as farmers or fishermen.

The Khmer people live on the western border,

A Montagnard woman (left) and a young Montagnard man (right)

near Cambodia. The Khmer are mostly farmers. The *Montagnards* (the French word for "mountain people") have many tribal groups, such as the Muong, Meo, and Tay.

19

The Chinese brought
Vietnam many new ideas
about government, religion,
science, and art. But the
Vietnamese people kept
their own way of life. They
remained different from
their Chinese rulers.

The Vietnamese finally took
control of their own land from
the Chinese in the year 939.
They named the kingdom
Dai Co Viet. For most of
the next 900 years, Dai

An 800-year-old Buddhist temple (left) in Vietnam. Dutch traders came to Vietnam in ships like these (above).

Co Viet was ruled by Vietnamese families.

In the 1500s, the Portuguese became the first Europeans to trade with the Vietnamese. Then, in 1636, Dutch traders came.

23

French warships attacking Saigon in the 1800s

FRENCH INDOCHINA

In the 1850s, the French wanted a colony in Indochina. By 1883, they controlled all of Vietnam, as well as Laos and Cambodia. They called their colony French Indochina.

The French set up large plantations to grow rubber trees, rice, and tea.

24

During World War II (1939-45), the Japanese army captured the French colony. Indochina's rubber, rice, and other crops were sent to Japan. But in 1945, the Japanese lost the war and left Indochina.

This government building in Hanoi was built by the French.

HO CHI MINH

The father of modern Vietnam was a Communist named Ho Chi Minh (1890-1969). He led the Vietnamese people against the Japanese and the French.

In 1945, Ho Chi Minh and his followers set up a new government called the Democratic Republic of Vietnam. Its capital was Hanoi.

Ho Chi Minh (right) is buried in this mausoleum in Hanoi. As a young man, Ho Chi Minh studied in French schools and traveled to France, the United States, the Soviet Union, and China.

But, in 1946, the French army returned to take control of Vietnam. In 1949, France set up a government in Saigon. Vietnam had a king, but he did what the French told him to do.

27

Ho Chi Minh and his
followers fought the French.
In 1954, they defeated
the French army at the
Battle of Dien Bien Phu, in
the northern part of Vietnam.

A peace conference was
held in Geneva, Switzerland.
The peace treaty split
Vietnam into two countries.
Ho Chi Minh led North
Vietnam, and Ngo Dinh
Diem led South Vietnam.

Diem ruled as a dictator.
In 1957, Communist
soldiers from South

Soldiers (left) patrolled the streets of Saigon in 1955, looking for Viet Cong forces. Ngo Dinh Diem (right) ruled South Vietnam.

Vietnam, called the Viet Cong, attacked Diem's soldiers. The Viet Cong wanted to put Diem out of power and form a Communist government in South Vietnam. Once again, there was war in Vietnam.

29

THE UNITED STATES IN VIETNAM

The United States did not want a Communist government in Vietnam. In 1961, President John F. Kennedy sent 16,000 United States troops to "advise and train" South Vietnamese soldiers.

So North Vietnam sent soldiers and weapons south to help the Viet Cong. This caused the United States to send more soldiers to South

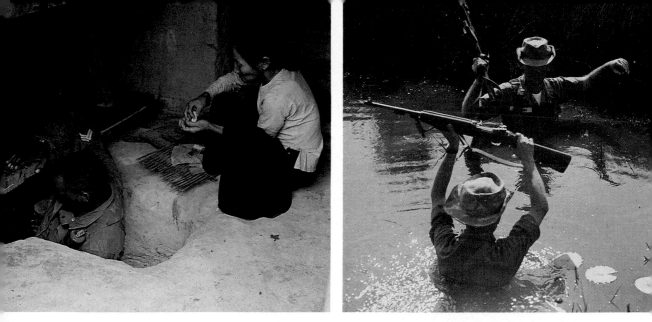

An American soldier looks for Viet Cong in a tunnel under a house in Saigon (left). An American officer trains a South Vietnamese soldier (right).

Vietnam. By 1967, there were more than half a million American troops in Vietnam.

The Vietnamese War was long and terrible. Both sides lost many lives. Finally, in January 1973, there was a cease-fire.

The North Vietnamese, the Viet Cong, the South Vietnamese, and the United States agreed to stop fighting. The last United States troops left Vietnam in March 1973.

But the Communists attacked again. On April 30, 1975, they captured Saigon, the capital of South Vietnam. The war was over. North Vietnam had won. The two Vietnams became one country.

Farmers use baskets and poles to carry their crops.
Fishermen use them to bring their catch to market.

LIVING IN VIETNAM

Vietnam has spent its money on weapons instead of on people. Its people are very poor. Most of them are farmers. They grow barely enough food to feed the Vietnamese people.

33

Rice paper (left) is made from the straw of rice plants. Woodcuts printed on rice paper are a popular art form. Concrete blocks (right) are formed in molds and then set out to dry.

There are not many factories. Workers make things by hand. Gradually the government is starting to build new industries. Industries provide jobs for people and products to sell.

Thatch-roofed houses in a country village

Most Vietnamese farmers live in small villages. Their houses are made of bamboo with palm leaf or straw roofs. In the south, many people live on boats near the rice fields or in

Houseboats in a crowded city harbor

city harbors. Most city
people live in small
houses built of brick or
stone with clay tile roofs.

Rice is the main food in
Vietnam, and vegetables
are included in many
dishes. Meat and fish are

scarce and expensive.
They are served in soups
or in very small pieces.

Vietnamese people wear
loose-fitting cotton clothing.
It is the most comfortable
way to dress in their hot,
humid climate.

The government does
not encourage religion, but
most Vietnamese practice
Buddhism. There are many
Buddhist temples in
Vietnam. Christianity, both
Protestant and Roman
Catholic, is also practiced.

EDUCATION

All Vietnamese children start school at five years of age. The classes are crowded, and there are not many books. The subjects include reading, writing, history, government, geography, mathematics, physical education, and home care.

Elementary school has five grades. Students go on to secondary school for

After the Vietnamese War ended, the government set up free schools for all children. Schools have very little science equipment, so young students do not study much science.

four more years. High-school graduates get the highest-paying jobs. Some students continue their education at universities in Vietnam or in other countries.

ARTS

Vietnamese artists are famous for their lacquer ware. Furniture, vases, and boxes are painted, then covered with many layers of clear, shiny varnish.

Left: Designs are sewn by hand on silk cloth.
Right: A craftsman with his colorful handmade masks

A lacquer-ware workshop in Ho Chi Minh City

Vietnamese jewelers make
beautiful gold jewelry.
   Vietnamese music is
played on drums, gongs,
and stringed instruments.
Many Vietnamese songs
are poems set to music.

41

HOLIDAYS AND RECREATION

Vietnam's Tet festival lasts for several days at the end of January. During Tet, people pay debts and settle problems with other people.

Vietnam Day is January 27. It celebrates the signing of the cease-fire agreement in 1973. On September 2, people honor Ho Chi Minh and the start of the Democratic

Republic of Vietnam in 1945.
For most Vietnamese
people, fishing, swimming,
and boating are skills
used in work as well as
play. People in Vietnam
have to work hard to

A farmer poles his boat through a rice paddy.

Transportation (left) and a magazine
stand (right) in Ho Chi Minh City.

make a living, and they
have very little time off.
Sports are not important
activities in Vietnam.
Instead, the people use
their time to make their
lives better and more
44 interesting.

TOWARD THE FUTURE

For thousands of years, wars and foreign rulers made life very hard for the people of Vietnam. But today, there is peace, and the Vietnamese rule their own country. The people of Vietnam are working to make their new nation a better place to live.

About the Author

Karen Jacobsen is a graduate of the University of Connecticut and Syracuse University. She has been a teacher and is a writer. She likes to find out about interesting subjects and then write about them.